Volume 1
Decodable
Reader

Mc Graw Hill Education

Bothell, WA • Chicago, IL • Columbus, OH • New York, NY

Contents

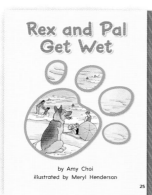

Pat and Dad

by Rose Whitman

illustrated by Susanne DeMarco

Pat is a cat.
Pat can nap.

Pat can bat.
Pat can tap.

Pat taps a hat.
Pat bats a pan.

Is Dad mad at Pat?

Pat ran, ran, ran!

Where is Pat?

Pat is on a lap.
Dad is not mad at Pat!

Hit or Miss

by Rob Rodriguez

illustrated by Anna Cota Robles

This is Bill and Kit.
Bill and Kit will hit.

Bill has a big mitt.
Kit has a big mitt.
The mitts fit.

Kit has a bat.
Bill has a bat.

Did Kit miss?
Did Bill miss?

Kit hit it!
Bill hit it!

Did Bill win?
Did Kit win?
Bill and Kit did!

Max and Tom

by Becca Fisher

illustrated by Rachel Ivanyi

Max is on a log.
What will Max do?
Max will hop, hop, hop!

Max hops off his log.
Max hops over a box.
Max hops a lot!

Max is back on his log.
Who can Max hop with?
Can Tom hop?

Tom hops off a log.
Max hops off a log.
Max and Tom hop, hop, hop!

Max can see jam.
Max hops to the top.
Max likes jam a lot!

Max has jam for Tom.
Max and Tom like jam.
Max and Tom can hop.
Max and Tom are pals!

Rex and Pal Get Wet

by Amy Choi

illustrated by Meryl Henderson

Ted has a pet.
His pet is Pal.
Pal is a big dog.

Ted and Pal look.
What can they see?

It is a man in a hat.
He has a pet.
His pet is Rex.
Rex is a little dog.

Rex fell in!
Rex will get wet.

"Help!" yells the man.
Pal jumps in.
Pal gets wet.
Will Pal get Rex?

Yes! Pal did get Rex.
Ted is glad.
Pal is a good pet!

Fun for Pug

by Tanya Wright

illustrated by Meg McLean

Pop and Tess have a big pig.
The big pig is Pug.
Pug likes fun.

Pug runs and runs.
Pug makes a big mess.
But Pug has fun.

Pug runs for fun.
But it is not fun for Pop.

Pop gets up.
But Pug hops up.
Pop can not get Pug.

Pug is not in his pigpen.
Pug runs in the mud.
Pug can go zigzag.

Tess tugs on Pug.
Tess gets Pug!
"Good job!" yells Pop.

"That was not fun!" says Tess.
Pug has a big grin.
It was fun for Pug!

A Fun Pet

by Eduardo Steinberg
illustrated by Deborah Colvin Borgo

Is a pup a fun pet?
What can pups do?
Pups can get wet in a tub.
Pups can jump up.

Pups can tip cans.
Pups can make big messes!

Mom puts the pups in bed.
Will pups nap?

Pups will not nap!
Pups will tug in a rug.
Pups will get on top of pups.

46

Pups yip and yap.
Pups kick and jump.

What can pups do?
Pups can sit on a lap.
Pups can give kisses!
Yes! A pup is a fun pet!

Volume 1

Decodable Words

Target Phonics Elements: Short *a, e, i, o, u*
*bed, can, cans, fun, get, in, is, kisses, lap, messes, nap,
not, pet, pup, pups, rug, sit, tip, top, tub, tug, up, wet,
will, yap, yes, yip*

High-Frequency Words

Review: *and, do, give, jump, make, of, puts, the, what*

Decoding skills taught to date:

Phonics: Short *a*; Short *i*; Short *o*; Short *e*; Short *u*

Structural Analysis: Plural Nouns -*s*; Inflectional Ending -*s*; Plural Nouns -*es*; Inflectional Ending -*es*; Closed Syllables